At Quarry Farm

At Quarry Farm

Poems by

James Plath

© 2025 James Plath. All rights reserved.
This material may not be reproduced in any form, published,
reprinted, recorded, performed, broadcast,
rewritten, or redistributed without
the explicit permission of James Plath.
All such actions are strictly prohibited by law.

Cover design by Shay Culligan
Cover image "Mark Twain's Quarry Farm Bedroom"
by James Plath
Author photo by Audrey Peterson

ISBN: 978-1-63980-754-3
Library of Congress Control Number: 2025939902

Kelsay Books
502 South 1040 East, A-119
American Fork, Utah 84003
Kelsaybooks.com

*Dedicated to Samuel and Olivia Clemens,
Susan and Theodore Crane, Jervis Langdon,
Mary Ann Cord, John T. Lewis, Jervis Langdon Jr.,
the Clemens girls, and other spirits
of family and friends whose presence
is still felt at Quarry Farm in Elmira, N.Y.*

Acknowledgments

The author is grateful for a two-week residency at Quarry Farm, the place where Mark Twain wrote his best-known works, and to the sponsor of the residency, the Center for Mark Twain Studies. Thanks are also due the Farm's Joe Lemak and Steve Webb, for their generosity and accommodation; to Sam and Susy Clemens for stories/language found in "The Barn: Still Life" and "Not Too Formal;" to Illinois Wesleyan University, for the sabbatical that made a fall residency possible; to the Colwell family, whose generous support of the R. Forrest Colwell Endowed Chair continues to enable research and writing; and to first readers Zarina Mullan Plath and Joanne Diaz, whose suggestions made the book stronger.

The author is also grateful to the editors of publications in which early versions of these poems first appeared:

Dear Friends: 2024 Year in Review (Center for Mark Twain Studies): "Never the Twain," "Reset," "Bad Company," "Parlor Games," "Spiritualism," "Break Fast," "On the Porch"
The RavensPerch: "Blank Slate," "Deer Watch," "Watkins Glen," "Cisterns"

Contents

Solitary	13
Bad Company	14
Reset	15
Break Fast	16
Of the Realm	18
Blank Slate	19
Never the Twain	21
Roughing It	22
Rabbit Holes	24
Living with Twain	26
Object Lesson	27
Muster	30
Half-Napping in Mark Twain's Bedroom	32
Spiritualism	34
Entente	37
On the Porch	40
The Barn: Still Life	42
Cisterns	45
Twain's Study	47
Our Lady of the Flowers	48
The Poor Girl	49
Not Too Formal	51
Parlor Games	53
Trick Shots	55
Victorian Table	58
Poor Huck	60
Deer Watch	62
Watkins Glen	63
Carved Stone Troughs	65
Family Plot	66
Retrospect	69
Residuals	70
Eclipse	71

"If these mute stones could speak,
what tales they could tell,
what pictures they could describe. . . ."

—Mark Twain, *Roughing It,* Book 2, Chapter 23

Solitary

This is my Walden, first time alone
in stitched silence so thick it hangs
like a mantle of pressing obligation
to do something, be something,
solve something, *think* something.

I'll admit, there is music in silence—
not my tinnitus, but a fuller toned,
thoughtful, deep-throated bassoon
or didgeridoo that wants to believe
in a higher power.

Solitude was a spigot for the stories
Twain drew from the headwaters
of memory, but he also enjoyed
the farm's cats as companions
before comfort animals had a name.

I'm allergic to cats, and my two rescue
dogs are too far away to rescue me
from seclusion here, where silence
and remoteness only amplify
already blaring imperatives.

Bad Company

To be the only one alive
in an old house that's dead
is unsettling, especially
on Halloween weekend.

Radiators make for poor
company, each clank an
invader somewhere in the
house; cold peers through

keyholes, darkness penetrates
thoughts—you're the sock
in the dryer that disappears,
and there's no help

in remembering the Gilded
Age baron who bought this
house had died a year later,
couldn't really enjoy it

with family he loved. Is it he
that I sense in unsettling
gloom, or am I my own
worst companion?

Reset

This morning I set the microwave clock
behind one hour. I am sensitive
to time in a place such as this,
an intruder from the present, each step
a trespass. The first-floor rooms
here and everything in them droop
heavy with history and no match
I can strike could impress those
who lived here once upon a time.

It seems I am always encroaching.

No knock on the head transported
me here; I came willingly, hoping
Twain's past would rub off
on my dwindling present. Here
I'm distracted, not by fair maiden
or errant squire, but by the gap
between people alive then and now,
wondering if evolution is still
on the right track, or if total
solitude ever was good.

This evening is exactly like the morning;
I am becoming one of them.
The key-wound Regulator on the wall
has been stuck since God knows when
at quarter to twelve. Outside, trees
bend toward panes of wavy glass,
as if listening for some sort of life
inside this metronomic mansion.

Midnight is always approaching.

Break Fast

Old house radiators always clank,
but at Quarry Farm
they're mostly nocturnal—deep
forest owls that swoop across
meadows of sleep; by morning,
it turns out, they're tired too.
Haunting is a full-time job.

In the kitchen, I toast myself awake
at the very table where Twain
began mornings, stretching
maples outside the window, the day
breezy, but sunny side up. Of course
he'd be a ham-and-eggs kind of guy,
not some mealymouthed cereal-eater!

An 1860s cast-iron stove still hulks
floor-to-ceiling, custom-made for beloved
cook Mary Ann Cord, an imposing woman,
sixty-five years a slave. Her story
of separation from husband, seven children
still hangs in the air, her presence
here strong and stirring as Twain's.

I like to think he engaged "Auntie Cord"
in chatter because of an egalitarian nature,
not to mine her gold with more success
than he had as a young man with Carson
City silver. In this abolitionist house,
both cook and patriarch had been
conductors on the Underground,

one of them even sheltering northbound
Frederick Douglass. Staring at this
iron monolith over jitter-free coffee,
I can't help but think how breakfast here
feels like Sunday: full of reverence,
heavy with martyrdom, bright with
stubborn faith and inspiration.

Of the Realm

Inside the butler's pantry that connects
the kitchen to the rest of the home,
a massive silver double sink rejects
the notion of rustic charm: inverted dome

times two that bear the hammer prints
on melted coins, reshaped by hands deft
since colonial times. The sink, with its glints
of morning sun, has a pedigree bereft

of caution that drove the rich to convert
their caches into harder-to-steal houseware
objects. This double beauty show of overt
wealth was moved from the private railroad car

of Twain's great-nephew, who, settling here,
turned it into one king-sized souvenir.

Blank Slate

At the top of the hill
where Twain would write
for twenty-some summers,
the wind has a voice,

and in the distance, vague
echoes of life being lived
in the valley below. Sound,
like heat, rises and the music

of solitude here is no solo,
but an unrehearsed orchestra
of notes, both natural and not.
I rest on a bench positioned

precisely where Twain conducted
himself as a writer, his study
watching over the city distant.
Pieces of slate from a rubble

foundation for the study
remain—still more shards
congregating under the chill.
Twain wrote mostly in heat

that demanded he open windows
to get a cross-draft blowing
across first drafts he anchored
with books as weights.

In his time, the study was
a cottage deep in the woods,
a living, vine-covered archetype
with stone steps at the end of a path

that wound past daisies, eyebrights,
brown-eyed Susans, buttercups,
and clover blossoms. Even in cold
autumn, with the earth hidden

by dead leaves and bony tree
branches beckoning like those
in cautionary tales, there remains
a fairytale hint of magic. I think I need

to hike here again when I'm not
distracted by those architectonic
fragments and the white
noise of first impressions.

Never the Twain

As I write, wind kneads
the upstairs windows so roughly
that any half-baked thoughts I have
fall flat. If Twain were alive, maybe
we'd tap that secret stash of beer
he hid, not well enough, in the house

of a temperance woman who tempered
expectations as sister Livy
and her family summered
each year after their father died—
a promise Twain kept joyfully,
his love of place walking hand-in-hand.

When he wrote *Roughing It*
in Susan Crane's parlor, Twain's vice
of choice was cigars, chain smoked
as he scrawled, puffing away
on a twenty-to-thirty-a-day habit.
Whatever signals were in those

smoke rings, any nuggets
of *wisdom detritus* are gone, as was Twain
in a puff of smoke after "Saint Susan"
constructed a gazebo-like study
for him to work *in quiet* on the next
ridge—far, far away from the house.

Roughing It

I've been out West—even
panned for gold in California
and killed a rattlesnake headed
my way. Been shot at twice
but never stood toe-to-toe
with an outlaw, unless mirrors
count. And maybe I shouldn't
have streaked that night
on a whim and a bet, but two
days in jail was as close
as I came to being a bad man
living in badlands—except
if raiding a Utah turkey farm
counts, or leaving a friend
to hitchhike home with a deer
rifle, wearing a bright orange
vest, after he cursed at me
from the top of a ridge. Soul
searching never does any
good when your soul isn't
wanting to be found.
I imagine that's how Twain
felt recalling his own stories
in the parlor of a home where
refined people only tolerated
his controlled burn and boozing,
his Old West style
cussing. Chuffing a mile
and a half up the hill
to the Farm and leaving
a locomotive trail of smoke

behind him, while the rest
of the family cared for his ailing
wife at the mansion in town,
he was roughing it all over again.
But so, I imagine, were they.

Rabbit Holes

Given a choice, the human
psyche will always hug
the stuffing out of tedium

until its bellyful of congruence
bursts like a piñata,
always drawing closer

to darkness that holds
the promise of a single torch.
At Quarry Farm, with its

cavernous mood, every room,
every object is a warren that
warrants immediate attention.

A look inside the old "cold"
kitchen leads me to open each
door, pondering the life

of ice boxes, a flurry of googling
when my task was to track
Twain's convoluted path

to celebrity. I crawled
down hole after hole, chasing
after cast iron, dairies, mediums,

abolitionists, silversmiths—
even Pottier & Stymus furniture.
It's hard to write where Twain

held court with a stogie for a scepter
and the world for an orb. Though
he never outgrew his essential

cravings or curiosity, here
he was somehow immune
to distraction. Or maybe family

time, porch time, time off
for good behavior to play
billiards were enough for him

to keep giving his public
the distractions they didn't know
how desperately needed.

Living with Twain

He's here somewhere, for if you trust
in heaven then you must also believe
in spirits. And wouldn't it be just
like Sam C., who would gleefully relieve

himself of any social custom, to thumb
his nose at finality, refusing to leave
his world of tall tales and vices—not succumb,
even if his lot of late had been to grieve?

Could it be *his* presence I feel here
in rooms hardly changed from the weave
of family, work, and play at Quarry Farm, where
he struck gold, managed to overachieve?

Aswirl, gold catches in a watery pan;
belief is catch as catch can.

Object Lesson

The list of dos and don'ts
for residents is shockingly brief, mostly
common sense: use the back door
spring or fall to keep from tracking
in leaves and crud; keep the kitchen door
closed to protect treasures from odors
and fumes; leave the thermostat set at 65
(optimal for preservation); limit use
of books from Jervis Langdon's library;
don't use chairs and tables with warning
signs; and remember, the general
public isn't allowed inside.

Then you're handed the key
to this living, breathing
museum where you alone
will reside the next two weeks.

You start out respectful, tipping
a hat when you pass by books
on any shelf, genuflecting in the presence
of objects resting on pedestals,
saluting portraits of American genius,
fighting back an impulse to curtsy
in the presence of all the fine china
you imagine stacked inside cabinets,
even tiptoeing around in house slippers,
leaving shoes in the first floor's only
livable room, where you treat tumblers
and mugs behind glass cabinet doors
as if they were imported crystal.

Then curiosity begins, erodes further
self-imposed *don't*s and suddenly you're
scooching up an approved chair to write
briefly on Twain's walnut table.
At least you don't sit in his favorite
parlor chair—not longer than a few
seconds, anyway, and you're careful
to write on a thick pad, leave no trace.
But you feel guilty all the same, till
your curiosity sends you back
to the library just to have another look
at a wooden cigar box labeled
from Quarry Farm c. 1920.

Then you remove the card
and lay it down carefully
before opening the lid, as if
trying to disarm a bomb.

Inside, you see two rolled Mark Twains
placed at a diagonal with labels up,
and you perceive, instantly, that caretakers
knew you would open that box—expected it,
even, since the smokes were newer
and carefully arranged. Next, an explosion
of recollections: the display of milk bottles
from Quarry Farm Dairy in the cold
kitchen and their docketed history, a placard
explaining the dining set, and dozens
more objects arranged for the benefit
of an appreciative audience of only one.

Then you realize you are free
to explore and discover, to find
inspiration in this living museum—
wherever you dare to look.

Muster

No suitor is ever good enough for any father—
trust me, I know—and Jervis Langdon was
used to getting his way. The coal and lumber
baron built the biggest mansion in Elmira,

met head-on the prospect of a prospective
son-in-law that came with baggage—no visible
means of supporting Livy, besides scant income
from writing or lectures. Worse, the man was

a "humorist," while Langdon was so serious
an abolitionist that he built Park Church, hired
firebrand preacher Thomas Beecher—whose sister
wrote *Uncle Tom's Cabin*—because

his old church wasn't abolitionist *enough*.
How he became an ally in the matter
of bringing his frail daughter and Sam Clemens
together is a novel, not a story, much less

a poem—and, as it turned out, a debt repaid
sooner than anyone wanted. Sam nursed him
during his steep decline, just six months
after he gave Sam and Livy the wedding gift

of a house, complete with maid, cook
and coachman. It didn't matter that, when Sam
was looking into buying a newspaper, Langdon
pushed Buffalo so his daughter would be just

four hours away, or that he went with him
to inspect the *Express* to make sure
the investment was sound. It was
all show, for he had already appraised

him, accepted him, flaws and all. He *liked*
Twain, and like and love come with their own
set of unreasonable expectations. Although
Langdon would have been horrified to learn

his mansion would be demolished decades
later to make way for a strip mall, statues
of Twain and Livy stand tall, still,
on the campus of Elmira College.

In the chapel, too, like saints, the couple
abides in separate stained-glass windows
that celebrate one man's righteous
intuition, as much as anything else.

Half-Napping in Mark Twain's Bedroom

The bedrooms of others inspire quiet,
reverence even—whether there's a whiff
of the illicit, a bouquet of fame, or a lingering haze

of the mundane—especially in older houses,
where the past is a building never to be razed.
Before hospice care, people expired right

where they perspired to start new lives. Old
houses hold all the glittering secrets a chest
so large can contain. Maybe that's why

it's always *so-and-so slept here,* not
*so-and-so ate here, laughed here,
shouted here.* Because someone asleep,

Twain, let's say, is most vulnerable
or close as he'll come to humanity
in its purest, most universal state.

Aren't sleeping babies at their sweetest,
while even slumbering adults betray
no grating habits, impulses, or prejudices

to irritate or unnerve? Twain awake
was a planet of unpredictable patterns
of sunshine, mist, thunderclaps,

and rainbows. Even here, during twenty
of his happiest summers, after working
all day he'd come down from the mount

maybe feeling like Moses, ready to read
them a few commandments or break
a few, even frolic with the cats or blow

smoke-filled soap bubbles again for the girls,
he could still be irritable. In sleep,
a person can do no good and no harm—

a comfort for others, like the relief that comes
when an annoying wind-up toy finally
winds down or breaks: merciful mitigation!

Maybe that's it: bedrooms and their suggestion
of temporary repose remind us, subconsciously,
of permanent rest—even at party houses, where

those rooms are still curiously hushed and coats
end up in a communal jumble that might as well
come with an iron fence and caretaker.

Spiritualism

Sam and Livy embraced
spiritualism after his favorite
daughter died at twenty-four

when he and Livy were abroad.
Only the sister-in-law he adored
was bedside with Susy, who

prayed, as a child, not to God,
but that there might *be* a God,
and if so, a heaven. It took a second

child's death to bring them
to that door, as it is hard to hug
a spirit. Scholars before me

living alone at Quarry Farm reportedly
felt Twain's benevolent ghost. If so,
he must have liked them more

than me, their projects better than
mine. Or maybe the random chills
I feel each night in this darkened house

are another spirit, or a Plato's cave
projection of my own inmost
nemeses. When I was a boy

I had kindred chills when forced
to fetch something from our Chicago
basement. I would pull the chains

on every light until I reached
the pitch-blooming pantry, grab a can
of whatever, then sprint past

the dark, pulling chains behind me,
steps to safety coming two at a time.
Now, nearing Susy's final age, my

daughter is a firm believer in ghosts.
On the phone she says she saw
two men in our last house, heads

topped with derbies and smudges
on their faces, standing just inside
her bedroom. She had told her mother

at the time, but it was news to me and
I told her when I was researching
I learned our 1906 house was occupied

by one of two brothers who owned
a coal company. And yes, bowler hats
were popular back then. She shrieked.

I almost did too, because that story was
Number 3 for me, and once is incidence,
twice coincidence, three times a pattern.

As a boy I was skeptical when my
grandmother told us about her father
stumbling home drunk and, in the same

kitchen by the same sink where
my brother and I took turns washing
dishes, he took God's name in vain.

Great-grandmother said he *dasn't* talk
like that or God will punish him, but
he railed "There IS no God." Just then

he pulled his hand from a trouser pocket
and screamed, because it was aflame.
They held his hand under water and pulled

his pants off. But the pockets were whole,
no hole, no charring. I took it as a cautionary
tale meant to curb my own four-alarm

language. Later, as a young man in the last
grandstand row at the Illinois State Fair,
wanting to be far from the maddening crowd

after working a booth all day, I felt a hand
on my shoulder (though no one was near)
and the gentle thought my girlfriend was

cheating. I phoned and got some sob story
about a friend of a friend and spending
the night, didn't want it to happen. That

was the second time, but apparently
it took a third to convince me, *yes,* there are
spirits: close and as distant as those still alive.

Entente

Saturday morning television
was my Mississippi River, a same
but varied, never-ending flow
of stories and adventures that became
my guide to life as I knew it.

I remember, still, an intro
to commercials on the campy
Rocky and Bullwinkle show,
the moose dressed like a swami,
hands hovering over a crystal ball:

Eenie Beanie, Chili Beanie,
the spirits are about to speak!

Are they friendly spirits?
the flying squirrel asks.

Friendly? Just listen . . .
Cut to commercial.

It's rattling around my mind now
like a marble on a roulette wheel
because I've landed on a spirit
problem I need to solve or remain
unsettled after dark as the child

I once was. At first I thought it
random when I felt a chill passing
from one upstairs work space
to another, like the reverse horror
of wading through a patch of warm

water in a public pool. Smells
followed and I googled my memory
to recall sweet cigar smoke; not
even cheap ones smacked of fried
potatoes. Could it be the cook?

In *Scooby-Doo!* mysteries the ghost
was always the caretaker, and the one
here raised his hand: Probably him
cooking in an adjacent apartment.
At 10pm? No, he said, adding

if it was a spirit his money was on Twain's
sister-in-law. After all, it *was* her house,
and I was sleeping in her bedroom.
Or maybe it's not a person at all.
Twain's daughter did say, "Everything

here is so full of the past—the cherry tree,
the air the odors the sounds of summer
every thing is so suggestive of a time
long ago, that one feels overwhelmed
with a cloud of sorrow. At night

it almost seems unendurable."
At my own daughter's suggestion
I begin talking aloud, apologizing
for whatever I'd done to upend or offend,
even assuring, *Hey, I'll be gone in a week,*

but afterwards feeling sheepish
as the guy banging pots in the woods
because buddies had told him
it was how to bag snipe. Had I just
bamboozled myself? I doubt

my subconscious is clever
enough to stage such a ruse.
Saturday morning education
has its limits. So do I, and I wondered:
if music could be used drive loiterers

from malls, why not here?
Alison Krauss soothes my own
restless spirit, so I fired off a few
rounds; afterwards, no pass-through
chills, olfactory tricks, no haunting,

and not a single poof of paranoia. Next
night I reloaded with Gloria Estefan
singing in Spanish, wondering if the now
calmed spirit might be music-lover Clara
Clemens. But once the episodes

had stopped altogether, the *who* became
irrelevant as the third-act unmasking
in *Scooby-Doo!* What mattered more
was that, without really communicating,
we had reached an understanding.

On the Porch

Old houses, new museums are always
cold, but there are plants inside determined
to thrive—you can tell by the attentive,
bright new growth. On the porch, autumn's
chill makes warm tea feel hot, even
as the air conspires to evaporate
the mirage. The only constant is the view,
nearly the same since Sam Clemens rocked
here while reading his daily output
to family—a view that, with little
adjustment by nature, seems precious
and permanent as a Wyeth, or Cole.

The gently sloping porch leads the eye
to a scene that seems to hang on a wall,
framed on each side by two stately sugar
maples, the bottom horizontal a linear
road rimmed by a squat stone wall.
This enormous *plein air* is dense
with hardwoods in a middle distance
that almost hide the Chemung River Valley,
while scattered behind them are bright daubs
of paint that hint of houses—pops of color
across a textured vista waiting for the arrival
of a bird, or balloon.

The star of any landscape is the vanishing point,
where parallel lines converge on a horizon
that seems almost as caught up in the process
as admirers. Here, a backdrop of Pennsylvania hills,
gliding and dipping gently as ballroom dancers
on the lawn, lead the eye toward a quiet,
unrehearsed splendor: sky that is not sky,
but an ocean-blue suggestion of more peaks
and ascents that continue indefinitely, a promise
that beyond this distant point of convergence,
beyond the hills, there is a place
that is even more peaceful.

The Barn: Still Life

I.

The notched opening on the single door
closest to the house was just small enough
for the farm's eleven cats to come and go
as they please, whether dining in or opting
for carry-out. If any were fat and lazy, Sam
made them so, especially ones he named
Sour Mash and Famine, who kept him
company many days in his study. Susy wrote
her father said if cholera ever comes,
he'd take Sour Mash to the mountains.

II.

Sounds coming from the barn: whinnies
and neighs, gentle mooing, lots of clucks,
a few quacks, and braying from a donkey
Sam ordered especially for the girls
(who also had a pet calf). Is it any wonder
this getaway was their favorite place
on Earth? Their father joined them
when he called it a day, went to the barn
around six or so to look at the cows
or take turns riding the donkey
that threw him the only time he tried.
It was funny to the girls and ironic
to the mugwump that he should be
so mistreated by an animal that
became the Democrats' mascot
the same year the family began
Quarry Farming.

III.

Like the Clemens girls, our family summered
with another, so I understand what it meant
to trade concrete and congestion for rural
relief. Our retreat was a lake cottage where
we swam, rowed, hunted frogs and turtles,
water skied, and bantered with adults who
treated children differently when we were
all away from our homes and routines. Play
narrowed the gap between children and adults.

IV.

Because Livy was too sickly to walk much,
it was Sam who took the girls on hikes
and did silly things like performing
elaborate costumed games of charades
or organizing the cat parade which proceeded
annually from the barn. First came
Old Minnie, great mother of cats,
next Aunt Susan, Clara astride the donkey
with a bundle of cats, then Sam and Jean
holding hands, the remaining cats trailing,
scratching out performances for judges
Livy and Susy, the latter once
remarking, "The difference between
Papa and Mama is that Mama loves
morals and papa loves cats."

V.

The carriages that journeyed up and down
the steep hill were kept in the barn under
a loft with a staircase so narrow and rickety
that no one is allowed now to climb it. There's
no sneaking around it, unless you're a cat,
since the door is kept locked to protect
curiosities visitors can see only certain
times each year. Inside are relics
from the dairy, a Stereoscope, wooden frieze
scenes from *Huck Finn, Tom Sawyer,*
and enough of the house's history to satisfy
a public barred from the house itself.
But happily the barn obliges.

VI.

Barns have been reliably red for hundreds
of years, wedded to landscapes, faithfully
functional and accordingly more stable
than old houses people routinely rehab, raze
or redecorate beyond recognition.
Is there a more iconic structure or style?
I admire most the wide floorboards,
square nails, the clutter of ropes
and clatter of hooves that resound, still,
in silence, and the layers of paint atop skins
of old remedies like linseed oil, lime, iron
oxide, skimmed milk. Even the barns
that stand tall as Lincoln's stovepipe never
seem to get their due, but remain America's
best side: nostalgia in its purest form.

Cisterns

sound like growths that should be
removed, or an ancient technology left
behind by a superior otherworldly race.

Some people call them rain
barrels now, cupped hands
hoping to catch pure water

for garden use. At Quarry Farm
one sits like a monument
to American ingenuity and thrift,

so near the house that artists could
paint it from porch shade, and solid,
imposing as the imported Spanish

olive jar Hemingway had shipped
to his house in Key West to fashion
a fountain for his cats and local

fauna. This cauldron-shaped
copper cistern was unearthed
next to the barn, where it once

cradled water to sustain the Cranes
and their dairy cows. In Key West,
cisterns were made of molded

concrete, large rectangles that,
now exposed, are gentrified
swimming pools, small

but functionally indulgent
as spring-fed Japanese baths.
Like Duchamp's urinal turned

upside down, this cistern is art,
but without the pronouncement.
Migrating pink flamingoes,

sundials, gazing balls, or stone-
faced angels can't compete.
Its unremarkable beauty

comes from simple gratitude
for a large object cleaved
from purpose. It sits there now,

like an anchor in a Yankee
waterfront square, in the buff,
ready for the next artist's brush.

Twain's Study

No doubt the Clemens girls were jealous
of the cozy octagon and its three-sixty
windows, toasty fireplace, couch, and table
set—secluded in the canopy above Quarry
Farm as a treehouse fancy enough for tea.
Morning glories vined over the wooden
sides, opening, like Twain, in the mornings
and closing shop when they've called it a day.
Sometimes this woodland scene played out
with cats, furring and purring nearby.
Twain called it the "loveliest study" and it
no doubt was before he turned it into a giant
hookah in which smoke swirled like a forest
fire out of control—Tom and Huck,
the Connecticut Yankee, others born here
probably choking as they breeched.

Even with windows yawning, the girls said
the cloud was heavy enough to keep them away,
and maybe that was the point. It must have seemed
a factory, smokestacks churning for all the stories
manufactured here, Twain punching in and
punching out, maybe whistling his way down
the hill after hitting his fictive quota. His daughters
knew enough to just peek inside and be invited in
or told to go—one time straight to Aunt Susan,
who designed a playhouse just for them: *Ellersley,*
the girls named it, which sat a hundred yards
from the study and came with a stove, table, chairs,
and dishes—all the stuff of good housekeeping
cottages in the woods, but far enough away so
when Twain scribbled furiously until his pen
caught fire, the girls were a safe distance away.

Our Lady of the Flowers

The world can never have enough saints.
Get in line, the queue's not very long;
All it takes is a challenge to accept.

For sixty years Susan Crane prepared Park
Church communion and furnished flowers.
The world can never have enough saints.

When Civil War vets returned to squalor,
She marshaled an army of merciful relief.
All it takes is a challenge to accept.

Low-income, minority children's cries
Were no match for one woman's big purse.
The world can never have enough saints.

Widowed Susan said *yes* to producing milk
Germ-free at her dairy, squashing typhoid.
All it takes is a challenge to accept.

Busy people make time for solutions:
Drop the excuses and answer the call.
The world can never have enough saints.
All it takes is a challenge to accept.

The Poor Girl

In the painting, she watches
all who pass a bronze sister
sitting atop an Empire clock
in what was once the music room.

Frozen in a Vermeer-like pose
of routine, this poor girl is
ostensibly engaged in doing the wash
at a fountain, her face turned away

from the task and a wistful look
betraying how far from here
she really is; but the careful folds
of her dress and the necklace

and stacked headdress she wears,
ill-suited for laundry, attest she was
paid to pose—though the matter
of her disengagement and inner

calm is still genuine. Maybe
that's why Twain bought the painting
in Europe with his sister-in-law
in mind. Everything Susan Crane

did was honest and unvarnished,
worthy of trust and admiration.
Aristocratic herself, Susan at heart
was peasant stock, comfortable

among both rich and poor, a true
humanist who remained tolerant
and tranquil no matter what her
brother-in-law said or did to try

to get her to lose her temper. But
it was only a game. Twain loved
Susan, took long daily walks
with her, no doubt saw her serene

face in this canvas girl—both
of them adept at measuring life
so that something good was
always within reach.

Not Too Formal

Yes, there is ornate craftsmanship
here, like the beams that calculate
artistry by geometric shape,
the tongue-and-groove ceiling
boards alternating like traffic
at intersections, or the rug
from Turkey with its rare colors
marching in barely detectable
order, the ornamental lathe
turned legs of table and chairs
that trumpet finery, puffery even.

But that didn't stop the lady
of the house from inviting John T.
Lewis to sit on those chairs
by the dining room fireplace
so they could chat about pears
and apples he delivered to bring
her New Year's party to fruition.

The tenant farmer was family,
now, after stopping the runaway
horse and buggy of Susan and Livy's
sister-in-law and niece before it could
go to "smash and scatteration"
at the bottom of a steep gully
where East Hill road zigged
precipitously. After the horse
and buggy mishap, Lewis often sat
and talked inside the house—one
time in the kitchen with Auntie
Cord, Twain listening
just a horse's length away.

Well-read, Lewis loved to argue
religion and the family's devout cook
saw the reach of God's hand
in the incident. "Now let folks go on
saying there ain't no God!"
heard Twain, leaning closer
to the swinging butler's door.

"Lewis, the Lord sent you there
to stop that horse!" But Lewis sassed,
"Then who sent the *horse* there
in sich a shape?" From that,
the argument got louder and louder,
much to Twain's delight.

The door he listened through still
swings open, and the rug is the same
he and others trod that day.
In this room the family took all
their meals, and despite the decor,
how formal can any room be that's used
every day in the house Susan liked to call
Go As You Please Hall? Even the enormous
pocket window with its view of the porch
suggests unbounded freedom
from Victorian manners that were
doomed to fail here when family
and friends gathered to laugh
and tell stories in their own
carefully constructed insouciance.

Parlor Games

In the parlor, nothing, it seems,
was as it seems:

The tiny dropleaf walnut table
was really a desk Sam used for wordplay,
roughing it before the study was built
a full football field away.

The Victorian couch was a classroom
for Livy to school her girls in German
and history, English, and the notion
it was all fun as farm-play.

The rectangular rug was a circle
for storytelling, later a place
for Sam and Livy and their
hosts to play Whist by the fire.

The Minton fireplace with ceramic
scenes from Aesop's Fables
was really a favorite bedtime game,
an exercise in consensus, imagination.

The Twain girls loved challenging him
to tell a story from a tile they picked,
but it had to be *different* from Aesop,
irreverent enough to make Livy frown
before smiling.

Even the beamed chestnut ceiling likely
was turned into a game, the girls lying
back, as children do, pretending
that up is actually down.

And that big picture window? A pocket
door, really, slid open to move furniture
onto the cool porch, cheerful chaos
provoking afterwards the inevitable
high-spirited cravings for more.

Trick Shots

Like *naked* and *nude,* billiards
and pool are a matter of class.
European royals hunched over
pocketless tables before tramps
steamed abroad, while *pool*
connotes dim lights, late nights,
whiskey broken fingers, the name
itself derived from betting.

Twain used to walk two miles
to Elmira most Sundays
in holy pursuit of his favorite
pastime—mine too, back
when I carried my own
cuestick and could run twenty
balls without a miss, raising
tempers only once for "hustling."

The billiard table,
as a Sabbath-breaker, can beat
any coal-breaker in Pennsylvania
and give it 30 in the game.

In the early days of billiards,
whatever the wager, elephants
lost: one tusk
was needed to make eight
balls, the ivory dyed and numbered
as the elephants' days, had Fifteen—
Ball Pocket Pool not turned
on the wheel of popularity
into a game of street-corner
halls, artificial balls.

Quiet when shooting,
I can't imagine Twain
marinating in silence;
unsavory jokes had to bubble
forth with every crack
of the balls, perhaps
a wry smile when the word
shark who loved exactitude
hit a three-cushion shot, planned
or not—rare felt-top equivalent
to a hole in one—yet sad
recompense for all the misses.

*The game of billiards
has destroyed my naturally
sweet disposition.*

At his Hartford house, Twain
could play billiards any time he
wanted, though like the table
in the basement of my childhood
it first had to be cleared—
in Twain's case, of manuscript
pages from a novel in progress.
Flat surfaces are always blank
pages for expressionist clutter.

His "Christmas table" was a gift
from a wealthy friend, and photos
show Twain playing with the women
of the house and also a biographer
who had moved in to "continue
research," instead spending hours
around the table with Twain,
who was so serious a fan he went
to New York City to watch
world-famous champs play.

*I saw nothing there in the way
of science and art that was more
wonderful than shots which I had
seen Texas Tom make on the wavy
surface of that poor old wreck
in the perishing saloon at Jackass
Gulch forty years before*

His biographer said they played
three-ball and four-ball
carom, a little fifteen-ball,
but mostly games of Twain's
own device. He mainly won
because, more than anything,
writers are especially adept at making
and breaking their own rules.

Victorian Table

Flea market flippers might easily overlook
this unassuming table, with its drop leaves
and single drawer, a scarred walnut top
bearing the brunt of lit tobacco Twain
left smoldering, while he tried to write
what he couldn't at the busy Langdon house.

When he penned *Roughing It* in the house
at Quarry Farm, before his study on the overlook
was constructed, he hiked from Elmira to write
in the parlor's blanket of isolation, leaves
whisking outside the only stirring Twain
heard, apart from birds—the air cooler at the top

of East Hill, brisk as a pace he would try to top.
A friend from California joined him at the house,
but like toddlers in parallel play, he and Twain
mostly worked, yet found it hard to overlook
the farm's charm—and a game of cards still leaves
an abundance of productive time to write.

The weight of a boyhood Twain wanted to write
was supported by the sturdy walnut legs and top,
the legs planed on eight sides, and an octagon leaves
a trail of myths. Though the Chinese saw it as a house
of good luck and Christians transition, he would overlook
all that and see it as a rebirthing table for people Twain

knew from the Mississippi River days Twain
seemed to live for—as if he were compelled to write
about the hard flow of current and erosion we overlook
when we revisit our pasts. Though scarred, this smooth top,
some eighteen inches square, was big enough to house
a family, friend, and acquaintance tree with enough leaves

to spring-feed a lifetime of fiction. Eventually the leaves
of this table would lose their ability to rise to level, Twain
no doubt cursing as his pen skipped across a walnut house
so slightly askew. But while it lasted, what a joy to write
upon, what American craftsmanship to try to top,
and what better place to do it than on this overlook?

Now the table sits in the parlor again, far from the overlook,
retired to a corner with a lamp and photo of Twain on top:
stasis, where once he labored to find the exact words to write.

Poor Huck

It's not enough that he had to audition
first in another book before he could be
the hero of his own, or impressive enough
that essentially he had to rear himself?

Brought into this world
by a mustachioed midwife
on a piece of walnut tolerably
smaller than a pork-belly slab,

Huck continues to be mistreated
by the society he only wanted
to escape—mostly because he talked
like a boy from before the Civil War.

With a dead mother and a deadbeat
alcoholic abusive greedy controlling
father, Huck was an early latchkey
kid, if the cabin had had a decent lock.

So don't hold running away against
him. He wasn't the first kid to think
foster care and a complete lifestyle
one-eighty too weighty a change.

Freedom-loving Huck risked six months
in prison—longer, since he couldn't pay
the thousand-dollar fine—just to help another
human who happened to be a slave.

Heading *south* on the river with a runaway?
So what if geography wasn't his forte. That raft
gave readers the chance to see black and white
friends navigate society's shoals and strainers.

It was close call after closer call, but
all he gets for his trouble is a sequel
from the midwife and his picture
on a Chicago-made peanut-butter candy.

Deer Watch

Having missed the herd every day
thus far, I'm staked out, beer
and camera in hand, ears pricked,
ready for anything. My doors are
open, all creatures welcome,
and that goes double for the red
foxes said to visit the Farm.
In the distance, a woodpecker
taps waning light. Fall slows
things down, lowers the heart
rate, gets everything ready for the big
slumber. Even Twain may have
found it challenging to write
this time of year in the spot
where his study rested before it
was gifted and moved, because
of vandals, to Elmira College.
It breathes easily, now, by the campus
lake, around which groups of students
slowly make their way toward
classes—their wild lives on hold.

Watkins Glen

I.

Hiking at seventy-three, the next ridge
looks like the last if you allow yourself
to think how Twain, robust as he was,
died in bed at seventy-four.

As a young man you were able
to tackle mountains by the ankles, not
even deer trails needed for steep ascents,
and afterwards surfing down the scree.

Now you need a pair of hiking sticks
and trails that aren't too uneven or full
of loose rocks that can seem obstructive
as obstinate boulders standing their ground.

II.

This path takes no evasive action, though
leaf-hidden drops startle as much as watery
dips on Disney's pirate ride. Above me, in
a canopy I cannot see, birds peck at serenity.

When I lived in northern California, I hiked
several miles to Feather Falls, carrying a tired
toddler all the way—no bad knees then, or
rubbery legs inclined to surprise.

For days I've been mostly exploring
the aisles at Wegmans, stockpiling
indulgences that a rule-follower can
eat only in the kitchen or on the veranda.

III.

My hike is a sea change, escape from single-
minded purpose, fulfilling a need to insert
myself into spectacular scenes after looking
at them from the Quarry Farm porch.
A new sailing venture rejuvenated Twain
to the point of denial: *And I'm a young buck,*
he told the press, *over seventy-one years
young at that*—the first stage of five reactions

in patients informed they were dying.
But aren't we all terminal—entitled
to whatever creative, palliative
pretense seems needed?

IV.

When the telephone was invented, the press sought
the opinion of Twain, who said "Every time
I see or hear a new wonder like this I have to post-
pone my death right off." Newness has that effect.

I appreciate my novel surroundings, but I am not
stealthy. Animals give a berth needlessly wide,
and I too am surprised to hear wet twigs crunch,
given Twain's complaint about Cooper: *It is a restful*

*chapter in any book of his when somebody doesn't
step on a dry twig and alarm* folks for *two hundred
yards.* Laughing as I stumble, I wonder if anyone
can hear, or if I'm only another falling tree.

Carved Stone Troughs

John Updike saw himself in a dogwood tree
his parents planted the year he turned one.
Parents do such things. Twain's jeu d'esprit
led him to place four troughs in part-sun

along the Farm on East Hill road, so spaced
to revive tired horses, and with their carvings mark
the birth of four Clemens—who may have raced
later to see whose was used, while dogs would bark.

But when three of four children die before the father,
those troughs become hollowed-out markers that bear
the burden of emptiness, not crosses to inspire prayer
or reflection. It's a wonder that Twain continued to care,

funneling stone-cold grief into sage
satire, instead of yielding to alcohol and rage.

Family Plot

Jervis Langdon purchased a plot
large enough to accommodate his
proficient family a year after the South

surrendered. Endings were on his
mind, and the visionary set this plot
in motion when he died a year later,

followed soon after by grandchildren
he would meet only here.
No longer in death are families

close, unless they were born
into royalty, or else poor
enough to keep children living

at home, holding down jobs
instead of careers that pull
in different directions.

Back when churches reached
for the heavens architecturally,
survivors did the same for loved

ones, each monument a minor
competition, like ladies' hats
on Easter Sunday.

Most people now reside in brass
or ceramic canisters on knick-knack
shelves or boxed in the back

of a closet, sometimes swirling
alone in artsy glass spherical worlds
or strewn like seeds never to grow.

The Cranes and Langdons
believed in an afterlife, Twain
in a spirit world of less certainty.

None of them thought their lives
over when their bodies
were planted underground.

The family was close in life, and in death
they are still together, arranged at the
Langdon family plot as though sitting

around the dining room table again
at the mansion or summer
farmhouse retreat.

At Woodlawn Cemetery, signs
point the way to Elmira's stars:
the abolitionists, a Heisman Trophy

winner, and of course Mark Twain,
"the man in white" who continued
to travel, even in death.

Twain passed away at Stormfield
House in Connecticut, but his body
was moved to New York City

for a funeral at a Presbyterian church,
then moved again for another service
at the place where he wrote the most.

Forty-four states were crestfallen
that his final tour stopped at two, and visitors
to the Langdon graves might feel let down

that of twenty-one family markers, Twain's
is conspicuously plain, as if to suggest he
had nothing more to add to this plot:

He had said it all in his books that,
stacked, reach the height
of the tallest memorial here.

Retrospect

Quarry Farm, with its stories begging to be
 rediscovered in the folds and pockets of every
room, has a vibe all its own—a simultaneous view
 of work and life that compels you to look
at your own and somehow step up your game.
 Before leaving, I needed to check out

the Stereoscope in the barn, to see more
 closely how this six-foot peep-show monstrosity
with six 3D photos of Twain was constructed.
 The contraption is somehow both sturdy
and rickety, a long, heavy wooden triangular box
 supported by three spindly legs of wrought iron,

as if the Christian power of a trinity was behind
 the optical tricks that would morph into a carnival
attraction, six people paying a dime to gawk
 inside a peephole, taking turns to view all six.
I had never seen one before, and the marvel now
 was not the 3D—two images, left eye/right eye,

forced into one—but the burlesque side of American
 amusements. Long before Kinsella wrote "If you build
it, they will come," Twain contemporary P.T. Barnum was
 luring suckers into his tents. For a time, Hollywood tried
but failed to reel moviegoers in with 3D, but in retrospect,
 people always seem to do their best peeping in private.

Residuals

Short term, I remember all things
routine—acts of repetition elbowing
their way past the fray: like my kitchen

confinement, bare-bulb outpost,
the long trek with phone-flashlight
through viscous darkness, past antiquities

and the smell of old furniture and stories
upstairs to books, stacked on the arms
of a regal chair, my robe a knitted throw

left behind as an act of kindness
by an artist whose residency also
was shivery. Nighttime solitude

mostly stands out: the still
unsettling feeling that maybe I wasn't
alone. But why not first thoughts

of magic, the pure cohesive joy of being
a small gear inside a colossal timepiece
stopped, yet accurate? Later, maybe.

Memory is a big brother that picks on you
sometimes, but mostly looks out
for you, even if he's late to the party.

Big brother is the one who picks up a brush
and whitewashes your fence, so all you recall
afterwards is that beautiful picket smile.

Eclipse

Twain, like any great story,
was a solar halo
indistinguishable from the sun.

When a man enters this world
riding Halley's Comet and grabs
its tail on the way out, it's cosmic.

Astronomers all but said so
when they named a crater
on Mercury "Mark Twain."

Twain, who moved from east
to west and back again, was
a self-made, self-proclaimed revolutionist

whose kinetic life created its meaning
before existentialists decided
to do is *to be*. Change is motion,

motion is change, and (sorry Kipling),
ever the Twain shall meet.

About the Author

James Plath is the R. Forrest Colwell Endowed Chair and Professor of English at Illinois Wesleyan University, where he has taught American literature, creative writing, film, and journalism since 1988.

His poems have appeared in numerous literary journals, including *The North American Review, Apalachee Quarterly, ACM (Another Chicago Magazine), The Caribbean Writer, Kansas Quarterly,* and *Spillway.* He is the author of two chapbooks of poetry—*Courbet, on the Rocks* (White Eagle Coffee Store Press, 1994) and *Everything Shapes Itself to the Sea* (Finishing Line Press, 2017)—and is the author/editor of eight scholarly books, including two on Ernest Hemingway, two on John Updike, and one on *The 100 Greatest Literary Characters.* Now president of the John Updike Society, he took the lead in restoring the John Updike Childhood Home in Shillington, Pennsylvania and curating exhibits for the museum the *Wall Street Journal* called "a worthy site of literary pilgrimage."

Plath is the proud father of six and grandfather of seven—now ten, thanks to a blended family.

www.ingramcontent.com/pod-product-compliance
Lightning Source LLC
Chambersburg PA
CBHW031204160426
43193CB00008B/494